NEON PALMS
and Other Chautauqua Poems

By
Martin Willow

Dedication

Neon Palms ... and Other Chautauqua Poems is dedicated to my mother, Anne Reim Willow. She imbued me with a passion for lakes, forests and fishing. But, most of all, I treasure the selfless love and overwhelming affirmation with which she touched my heart. Mom, I will never forget you.

Acknowledgment

A very special thanks goes to Susan Schwaidelson Siegfried. Without her suggestions and editorial input, this book would suffer the faults of a myopic author. She is my invaluable muse in providing insight, skillful critique and corrections.

Contents

Addiction | November 2008

I am addicted to water
there is no other explanation
I am addicted to water
I can't get enough

Like a winnowing rod
my body aims towards a lake
eyes tethered to its magnetic blue
ears arching towards tuning fork wind
legs racing to waves that batter its bank

A lake is a universe tented by sky
cradle for the horizon
a stage where trees perform their dance
theater for otters of burlesque

I am captivated by oceans and seas
by whirlpools spinning into oblivion
and tides pursuing the moon,
when rains throw down gauntlets from the sky
rapture fills my chest

I am mesmerized by powerful thrusts
hurled against boulders holding firm
by streams trickling along cattails and reeds
and persuasive currents curling weeds below

⋮
∨

The crashing waterfall
at the edge of the world
a soothing nursery rhyme,
the swirling pool beneath
a goblet of glistening wine

I am addicted to water
I can't get enough
like a tree sucking life through its roots
I am a willow with insatiable thirst

Wealth | May 2008

My wealth is lake and wind
graceful courtship
power when they converge

My fortune is sky
inheritance secure
promise, hope
charity pure

Eagle, sun
mystifying clouds
endless poems
inspired by ascent

The wealthy are not those
with gold and precious jewels
but those who find creation's art
a gift of daily renewal

Behind Chautauqua Clouds | May 2008

Behind the clouds of night
are beings not seen by day,
wearing masks that blot the stars
they peer from ridges framing the sky

As moon rolls by
profiles can be seen
peaking through fissures of light
scanning the world below
marveling at the earthly realm

This is where the angels hide
observing as we move, love and sleep
slipping quietly into our world
to help and protect God's precious keep

Listening | January 2008

I go out onto the lake
to hear God

I hear waves
psalms spoken with heaven's tongue
I hear poems
gleaned from furrows of sun

I hear wind
breathing lyrics in my ear
and parables packed as cottonwood balls
mingling with the clouds

This is God's voice
a balm that heals a weary heart
and the drone of drums within
with images free of words
and grace absolving sin

I go out onto the lake
to hear God whisper

.

Month of Psychosis | June 2008

January and February
certain of their vocations
drape chilling shrouds
over the earth

Confused ...
March stalks us
a psychotic prophet
enticing us with promises
and dubious assurances of life

April Tempest | April 2014

A shark invaded this freshwater lake
his siren fin warning the shores
a tempest tore through its midsection
waves tossed like shards

A wild wind
shackling its back
cursed the night
mocking onlookers
anchored to land

Behind the shark
unseasonal sleet rode its wake
dumping their buckets
into the furrowed lake

As walls of snow
rolled over the horizon
flattening the land
the great white barred its teeth
in ominous grin

Spring | May 2008

In spring the hills are lime
the lake cresting eggshell white

Winds swirl in silver gowns
sunlight weaves a fabric of silk
for the arms of the red-jewel crab
embroidered with rubies and pearls
red berries and blossom

The golden cypress
guards a young iris of Siberian descent
tulips of empress pink
raise goblets filled with light

A chestnut squirrel
darts through an arbor vitae hedge
intent on retrieving
October's stash of nuts

Awake from hibernation
a raccoon takes his nightly stroll
through the yard, down to the lake
rummaging spring's early ground

⋮
v

Boats freed from shrink-wrap shrouds
that shielded them from the winter snow
are greeted by Chautauqua's embrace
as they ease into their slips

The magician of each year
Spring takes what is dead
bringing it to life
an alchemist turning lead to gold

Through the Leaves | March 2010

Thanks to May,
streets are cleaned
winter's mess raked off yards
each lawn given its first manicure

When June sneaks into town
trees open umbrellas against the sky
awnings of green
arches supporting the sun

But, in the few days between bursting
buds and countless leaves
the winking night comes alive
stars play hide and seek
amid trees drowsy with the dark

Oaks stir, animated giants
slow in the night
hickories tap canes
along spring's nocturnal lanes
their thin shrouds of green
studded with eyes that spy
my every move

Eyes inspect the night
watching from midnight's perch
cats purring in the mesh
whispering nothing
seeing everything

May | May 2008

The leaves have all turned out
to approve the day,
the lake swims with the sun
a prism of warming rays

A sixteen-foot Lund speeds by
headed for a crappie catch
a Pro-line open-bow
white with black ribs
takes its first run of the season

All through May
carp waggle in rendezvous of love,
behind them
the heartbreak of last year's kill

Bass and crappie
test warm shallows
winter-lean muskies follow behind
stealthily cruising
for an overdue meal

Other couples paddle along
surveying banks for the perfect place to nest
the chatter of ducks echo over the lake
maracas mingling with the wind

⋮
∨

May brings out the best of Chautauqua
water that is clear, trees expressing delight
wind stretching arms over the lake
motors forgotten in the night

This is the month
when all things
come to life

Raising a Glass | September 2008

From a lakeside berm
a Siberian iris with velvet hands
raises a glass
wild cabernet
toasting sunlight on waves

Bringing up Babies | April 2008

This year the lake in front of our house
is home for two feathered matrons
one with eight ducklings in tow
the other with more than ten

Each duckling follows close
as mother forages for food amid
vegetation floating in the shallows
refuse dismantled by the blades
of weed whacking vessels

Doing as mother does
the little ones wet their beaks
scooping up plankton, minnows
and other tiny swimmers that
dart beneath their paddling webs

Each mother leads her badling
up the lake's rocky bank
stopping halfway to poke
their fuzzy heads over the edge
to see if all is clear

Continuing up sixty feet of lawn
to our patio, they dine on breadcrumbs,
birdseed and the honey nut cheerios
my wife sets out for hungry fowl

⋮
v

The patio march repeats again and again
every morning, afternoon and evening;
my wife complying
to duckling demands

This ducky feast is followed by me
habitually chasing the family fowl
from the yard
down the rocky bank
back into the lake

Where little quackers will find … (I explain to my wife)
a more authentic diet – proteinaceous water bugs,
tasty algae, juicy grubs and more exercise
for their infant legs … (she doesn't buy it)

Where their shit falls to the lake bottom
not to the top of our lawn
where my lawnmower disperses it
as a fertilizing memento of their trek

The Surge | June 2014

The sky was slashed
June's barrel emptied

Roads were closed
cars stranded like
donkeys mired at their knees

Brown surge, mud and debris
bled into the Southern Bay
girding its mid-section
with a river of sludge
a mud jug
emptied from Chadakoin Creek

A snake loosed by the storm
half-mile anaconda
wallowing in the sun

Not even Chautauqua is impervious to
bedlam poached from serenity's hand

Like us, the lake waits it out
patient for the healing
that will purify and cleanse
content that tomorrow
is the redeemer of today

Tourist Season | October 2014

From Memorial Day
to Labor Day
they come
by the thousands

Tourists from Virginia
Ohio, Pennsylvania
visitors in search of escape

Hummers, Audis and Beemers
filled with brokers and corporate execs
honking their fame

In rites of attainment
the affluent remove tarps from
summer home windows,
strip shrink-wrap from
sleeping armadas

Putting in docks
boatlifts and moorings,
they prepare to take on the lake

Common folk flood campgrounds
motor homes stuffed to their tops
canoes strapped to their roofs
Weber grills ratcheted to bumpers

⋮
∨

All of them
simple or elite
come to launch their dreams
… in bass boats, MasterCrafts,
catamarans and kayaks,
thirty-seven foot cruisers
with bellies like whales,
jet skis racing the wind,
slim lasers skimming waves

Every July 4th night
they commandeer the lake
running lights dim against
explosions brightening the sky

In the short time they thrive
each finds magic on water
freedom in the wind,
green-eyed for the lucky ones
who call Chautauqua 'home'

Life Was Meant To Be Like This | July 2007

Put me in a boat at sunset
rolling with the waves
laughing with friends
trading legends of conquest
absolving weakness and woe

Put a fine cigar in my hand
a Liga Privada #9 I prefer
and a full red wine
life was meant to be like this

Startled by narrow visions
from our critics and wives,
we are calmed by companions we meet
… lake, sky and wind
… nature's menage-a-trois

As the lake rolls,
so too the time
and the wind
and the wine
cigar aroma, evening incense
night slides in

The moon raises a glass, tips his hat
our invited guest
life was meant to be like this

⋮
∨

Without reproach or regret
a Syrah spills onto the boat's gray carpet
marking forever the good times we had

For some of my friends
it is the purest of escape
from the purists and cruelest
they must call "friends"
for all of us it is all that is needed

And for one of us
it is the first time to
pee off the side of a boat

Children of God | November 2008

Tree limbs intertwine as arms
comforting each other's fears
songbird hymns soar on the wind
a gospel of peace for every ear

The blessing of bees pollinates the earth
tending gardens tender with care
caterpillars find magic in caskets of birth
dragonflies find romance in the air

When the Rain | September 2009

I like to be alone
in the pouring rain
a silken sheet of charm
coating my skin with calm

Violins with silvery tongues
play softy overhead
each note a platinum bead
suspended on a thread

Memory rustles like rain
through summer leaves above
I hear the flutter of wings
the songs of a wandering dove

I will remember you forever
if not each moment
I will remember you forever
in each drop melting into earth

When rain falls
upon dry deserted land
I follow footsteps charting hope
catching each drop
in a chalice of open hand

Man in Balloon | July 2008

He drifts among clouds
a hot air balloon
300,000 miles away

I think our moon enjoys
his ride through the day
sharing the sky with the sun
and boats riding the waves

Longing to be a gull
he dresses all in white
riding an air stream
high on the freedom of flight

Maybe there really is a man in moon
maneuvering his craft on helium gas
wandering above, a wizard in the sky
sipping sunbeam wine

In a few days
he'll escort the night
bigger and brighter
accompanied by Venus and stars
reminding us that
thousands of miles
and dreams in our eyes
aren't really so far

Outlines | December 2008

Liquid parchment
moving in rhythm and rhyme
choreographed mystery
performed in perfect mime

Hills outlining sky
clouds outlining rains
waves outlining wind
sails outlining freedom

Chautauqua is a scroll
engraved by passing time
a poem penned in silence
encryptions kneeling within its lines

Up and Down | March 2009

Chautauqua's moon triangulates
off the sailboat mast
whether the market is up or is down
whether or not the mortgage is paid

Rocking swells from passing boats
are memoirs of fortunes won, treasures lost
metronomes of opportunity
achievements true or false

Barn swallows skim the air
taking hold of a zephyr
not letting go

Eagles command the sky
circling high, almost out of sight
plummeting in defiant dives

Like the moon, like the waves
like birds strong in the wind
there are those who dream
and often attain

There are others
who go up and down
experiencing joy, confronting pain

These are the ones with the most to tell
those who risk beginning and end
these the ones I call my friends

Words Upon Chautauqua | November 2007

I have spoken my worries to the wind
clouds carry them away
I have tossed my sorrow to the waves
to be cleansed in clarity's spray

Frustration is quelled
by evening's soft hands
the future is seen
upon the long rolling land

Words come easy
when souls confront that which is pure
Chautauqua offers healing
gentle, unspoken cures

Cathedrals | June 2008

Haze spreads a net over Chautauqua
turning close green risers blue
and distant hills phantom pale

Ulrich's 38-footer tacks along the wind
main canvas full and tall
water churning a blueberry grey
in free bubble flow

Cathedral clouds
filled with saints adorned in radiant robes
passing in slow procession
tossing baskets of grace to us
waving as they go

Sunset | August 2008

A tree of fire rises from the lake's west edge
branches reach as tentacles to the sky
igniting clouds as if they were withered brush

Grabbing the horizon by the throat
an inferno is forced upon the lake
crimson flowing into its gut
waves lapping flames like drunks at last call

With wings flaring red
a thousand birds take flight
embers scattered in the sky
oblivious to the fiery night

Djembe on Chautauqua | September 2009

Sitting by the shore
he plays a solo to the night
hands flashing upon tightened goatskin
palms beating sonnets for the moon

Thundering thuds echo over the lake
a hollowed stump bellowing
its moan across the waves

A soul calling to tribes long gone
invoking an ancient lore
oneness with the land

Passions, dreams
rise from djembe rim
panthers leaping
upon Chautauqua wind

Flames in rhythmic flight
spirits of ritual dance
shadows in the night
held captive by the trance

Neighbors listen from porches
boats bounce with the beat
each captive to the music of the lake

All Along the Lake | August 2007

I know they are making love tonight
all along the lake
lights are dimmed, curtains pulled down

I see thoughts embracing love
finding beauty in old skins
landscapes where they have been before
each touch new on every hill

I see lips wander
calf to thigh
envelopes of surprise in every kiss
familiar positions
unfamiliar bliss

I know they are making love tonight
all along the lake
moonlight spreading its sheet
over rhythms of the night

Warning | September 2007

The west wind is strong tonight
the sky ragged with clouds
a thin sail torn without regard

Usually the evening quiets the day
but, tonight the air is different
it bodes tomorrow's storm
the colorless horizon
bares trouble for the morn

The lake heaves from within
months of suffering intense summer heat
centuries of anger stored deep beneath
its sediment cluttered with bones

This is Chautauqua's warning
to all who venture forth …
I will not be caged by human will,
I will not be tamed by human hands

Peeping Tom | July 2014

Even the sun tires of fame

Most days he's the conspicuous
big guy in the sky
but, every so often
he likes to play the spy

When grey clouds rush past
incited by impetuous wind
the sun is content, even delighted
to mask his identity
in a game of hide and seek

Not the bright star
in our cast of celestial celebrities
just a silver disk
mimicking a timid moon

I think I know why
he likes the masquerade,
his chance to play

Peeping Tom with monocle
staring through the grey
observing his earth
ninety-three million miles away

Dog Day | December 2008

Just before the ominous clouds
encircling Chautauqua
let loose their rain
the lake becomes flat
just like a dog's tongue
on a hot summer day
limp and lazy
its body lying still
waiting for the sky
to quench its thirst

Chautauqua Macho | August 2007

Docks everywhere
jutting their lumber
one hundred and twenty feet or more
into lady lake
the longer the better

Every lake house has one
wood braced with steel
a contest of length and pride
compensating sighs of the smallness of men

Raindrops | February 2013

Water sucked from Yangtze and Amazon
trickle from leaves in lakefront yards,
tumbling down banks into lake
Chautauqua swallows them
one with waters of the world

Stories of Mississippi, Susquehanna, Lake Erie
swim in shallows and springs of this Upstate lake,
music composed around the world
falls in raindrops from the clouds

A minstrel wind carries
ballads of foreign tongues
voices softly singing
librettos caressing the air
welcome songs from afar

Summer's shimmering boil
rises as vapor pools in the sky
convoying in clouds, circling the earth
returning gifts to a thousand lands
back into Yangtze and Amazon hands

Water endures through all of time
cycling secrets and sounds of life
generations gathering in pools of hope
a trillion voices becoming one

Casino on the Lake | September 2012

Not really a casino
oh, lots of money passing thru palms
but, none for slots or roulette

Just a good time bar
where the lake squeezes
its middle

Bemus Bay
by day a lakeside oasis
for sailors and pontoon parties,
when the sun goes down
a night owls' roost

Where everything happens
after 10 pm
girls in shorts so tight
they kill,
guys in tank tops
with tattoos displayed
alter egos flagging down applause

Casino jumping
to the beat of The Nerds
Smack Dab, Smokehouse
Only Humen, Jack the Dog
and Black Widow's sexy queen

⋮
v

Taps spew Bud Light and Labatt's
plastic cups spilling over
Red Bull and Vodka
dance floor slippery with the juice

Boats from North and South Bays
tether themselves to hitching posts
at each dock
all have come to drink, dance
and flare their skin

The Casino at Bemus Bay
the only place to go
since The Surf Club
changed hands and
sterilized the night

Idiots of the Lake | July 2008

It's 10 pm
the lake dark under
canopy of cloud
I'm alone in my boat
lights on

Only a few on the lake tonight
a lake one and a half miles wide
eighteen miles long
how quiet
no one else on the water

Suddenly, out of the darkness
comes this joker with a boat full of friends
all in party mode
he passes within twenty feet of me

My first urge ...
cast a musky lure at his port side
catch a rail, yank it hard
make him capsize

"Hey, jerk
my lights are on
you almost hit me"

⋮
v

During the day
jet skis infest like lice
mopeds splaying the lake
slicing waves
uprooting weeds
terrorizing bluegill and bass

No respect for fishermen
silently laboring at a catch
no regard for those relaxing
with rod and reel

The lake is large enough for us all,
so why do these idiots think
Chautauqua is only for them?

Firebird | October 2008

Holding eternity in talons of gold
an eagle soars into the setting sun
his eye a disk of fire

The sky is his and his alone
the world only a wayside
as he flies into destiny's arms

He is freedom to our desire
risk to all that burns within
the horizon he pursues
a birth from trial to glory

Bronco Busting | August 2008

Wild horse of a lake
bucking bronco with powder keg legs
a runaway refusing to be tamed

Charging with relentless rage
hooves pound the lake
whitecaps kicked
into my Sea Ray's sides

Nostrils flare
chest heaves with every snort
a manic wind commandeers the reins
of this stallion unbridled by man

I'll take this ride anytime,
a welcome pace amidst
the chaos of my other life

Neon Palms | September 2008

A sign of our times
sprouting on Chautauqua's banks,
Johnny Appleseed's electric progeny
the neon palm

There aren't too many yet
this is just the first planting
and though the banks are fertile
these trees have no roots in need of dirt

They grow from the ends of docks
from the concrete patios of lakeside yards
photosynthesis exchanged for a surge of electrons
bringing buds to life
delivering the telltale green
that defines them as trees

Across each bay
they rise from base lit blue
along stems glowing white,
unquenched by darkness
their emerald arms gush as
geysers of affluence on summer nights

When the switch is thrown
they appear as bartenders
at parties 'round the lake
serving margaritas as Chautauqua sways
to reggae and rock

⋮
∨

In a few years this tropical fad
could ring the lake like weeds
more enduring than milfoil
standing tall through snow, sleet and ice

Until then we'll watch a few more
appear each year
casting their artificial sheen upon the waves
a neon millennium drawing near

Good Cigars and Shooting Stars | August 2007

Many hearts were saddened
the Sunday you announced you would be leaving
you had a call from Seattle
your boyhood church beckoned you home

Seattle is where you belong
the Spirit bidding you on
Jamestown will be in the past

The future holds promise,
renewal and certain hope
the present is the moment
where God is to be found

For nearly seven years
you labored faithfully
prodding and plowing souls in need of repair
some received you with joy
others recoiled from the test

Though bruised you did not back down,
seeking reconciliation
with those who hurt you most

Water renews and replenishes
as it falls upon a land

⋮
v

For some, you were a torrential downpour
eroding years of comfort and crust
for others, a refreshing rain nurturing
new ideas and questions that provoke
… to all, you were a messenger of God

For you, water bid a welcome repose
those late night drifts upon the lake
restored your spirit
offering hope to a wounded soul

Something in the easy sway of waves
spoke to you about resting in God's will,
something in constellations of night
(despite our ability to name only a few)
caused you to marvel about his long reach
into lives like yours and mine

Lake Chautauqua will not be the same
it will miss the skipper navigating the night
with new found skill
skimming along its spine in a Sea Ray
under full moon

And your flock will not be the same
but surely better, because of a shepherd like you
encouraging a passion for essential truth
and the appreciation of parties and art

⋮
ᵛ

As for me,
I will remember smooth red wines
Johnnie Walker Black
trails of good cigars and shooting stars
in the richness of Chautauqua nights
and a good friend to share them with

May God's hand be upon you
all the days of your life

Where is the Wind? | June 2008

Where is the wind
when all is still?

When the lake becomes glass
without ripple or quiver
where does the wind go?

Is it sucked into the earth
retreating into burrows for rest?

Does it bow its head
close it eyes
waiting for the sun
to wake it from its sleep?

Does night have power
to pluck feathers from its wings?

An impotent stir
a mere shadow without breath
that is the wind when all is still
losing the will to thrive
the sky heavy on its chest

Orphans | July 2008

A trio of ducklings waddles through our yard
three little orphans banded together
abandoned and alone
something awful must have happened
to their mother

Each day bodies grow
bills get longer
webs get larger
wings come into their own

Each day they march
across the grass
to the bird feeder pole
picking up tidbits of seed and grain
that fall to the base
cautious, yet confident
we'll leave them alone

Next year we'll see them again
earlier in the spring, fully grown
skilled in the methods of flight
takeoffs, landings
each with a spouse looking for a home

Together they will parent
their own little brood
each wary of the danger
that left them alone

Rest | May 2014

After three days of wave-churning wind
Chautauqua has shut down for the night

Upon its sparkling mirror
starlight glimmers
a healing to the violence
that ripped and scarred

Made It | September 2008

I made it
I finally got away

Weary of the drone of rubber on concrete
and doing business in Rochester
Poughkeepsie, Albany and Syracuse all week
I finally made it

Within minutes of pulling into the driveway
changing clothes and gulping down a bit of dinner
I was on my boat
with paper and pen
Old Crow and a cigar
skimming the waves
right into Chautauqua's arms

Whether I succeed or fail
resist or succumb
it doesn't matter
for the lake doesn't judge
nor does it look for rewards
in the holes of my hands

It is there for me
to drift upon its waves
listening as it speaks
in tongues mysterious, yet known

⋮
v

Hanging onto every word
it tells me of all the things I wanted to be
and possibilities to come

Chautauqua my lifeboat
when love is lean
when love is grand …
the liquid center of the universe
an ocean of dreams outside my door
a rescue for the drowning man

I'll take 20 mph on the lake at night
over 75 on the Dewey Thruway any day

Gentleman of the Lake | September 2007

With stately posture, perfect poise
the gentleman of the lake
steps stealthily down the dock
his gaze intent upon
all that swirls below

He hides in broad daylight
mimicking lines of aged driftwood
morphing into weathered grains
of lake house piers
elegant against the teal green
of Chautauqua's rolling field

The Great Blue Heron's cane is a rapier beak
targeting any morsel wiggling with life
the tiny perch, the gaping clam
stabbing with precision
stilling them both

With wingspan cape
he leaps into the air
a kite riding the wind
the main attraction
on the boulevard sky

Clouds | September 2007

Clouds
language of the sky
exposing our lives
in bubble thought patrol

Cumulus revelation
balladeers of the air
collecting stories scrolling through time

Clouds carry messages from far away
hinting the world is one
and division an illusion

If only we could reach into the sky
snatch a cloud and slip it into our skulls
then would secrets unravel
and disparity disappear
as clouds become whispers in the dusk

Sundown | January 2008

Jets streak like meteors
before the setting sun
their trailing tails
cloaked in stratospheric clouds

Shadowy hills pitch their tents
trees close their eyes
leaves become bed rolls
folding inward

The sun's violet tongue
dips into the lake
sucking daylight
into the crater of night

Movements of Night | December 2007

The sky folds raven wings
over Chautauqua hills

A mossback musky furrows the lake
its dorsal fin leaving a rippling wake

Stars emerge as fireflies
from night's grey clouds
inscribing lights of other worlds
upon the solitude of dark

With simple steps
nocturnal songs
descending
from the moon
walk upon the water

Midnight Sun | October 2008

An Alaskan summer
has found its way to New York State
a midnight sun hangs its mirror
confusing this August night

The sky opens its kimono
just enough to tease voyeur eyes
traces of blue through vaporous skin
stars peeking from a moon glow robe

A photon elixir infuses
veins of surrounding trees
silver spears probe each leaf
fountains of oaks and maples
burst in emerald green

Chautauqua is half awake
unable to shut its eyes
gulls find it difficult to sleep
geese trumpet a choral insomnia
boaters douse their running lights

These hours have no need for sun
in the presence of anonymous dark,
this paradox no need for answers
when the moon is so stark

Howler | August 2009

Sucking oxygen from Chautauqua's lungs
a late night storm turns the lake inside out
its viscera heaved as chum upon the waves

A howler screeches out of the west
a cannibal hissing in the face of dark
cauldrons churning in thunderhead boil
severing flesh from anchors of bone

Turmoil shakes the world loose
skin, brains, legs, arms,
weeds, logs, frogs, geese
anything that creeps upon the ground
anything that tests the violence of the air

Small boats are flung as leaves shaken from a tree
flimsy frames tossed as dice into a gale
5 and 10 outboards belittled by the rage

Time has come to take cover
to underestimate, the crucial flaw
skin of man, parchment falling apart
pride bowing to the squall

Lightning | May 2008

Lightning crashes from the sky
scorching the lake with stinging prods

Veins of blanching blood
surge from Chautauqua's eye
silver spurs of electron storm
scratching at the darkened moon
etch themselves onto the gel-print night

Pitchfork barbs jolt the dark
x-ray bursts galvanizing fright,
skeleton trees stunned with fear
paralyzed in ghostly white

Shock waves burst
balls of terror
roll into Chautauqua's bed
manic winds swirl
with a madman at the helm

Blinding gusts of rain
plummet as havoc from above
pounding Chautauqua
with fists of hail
battering tender flesh

The lake is a frying pan
for boaters and beasts caught in the storm
petrified specks seized with alarm
faces of dread alone in the night

Concert Hall | April 2008

From the cradle of the sleeping sun
the quarter moon strums
silver notes on strings of light

The Milky Way cloaks celestial choirs
singing arias in the night
its starburst symphonies
brilliant in their flight

In this concert hall of night
the sky unrolls a lullaby score
a soft blanket of music and light
where the soul flies in search of clarity

Clouds of Night | September 2007

Are there secrets in the clouds of night?
secrets hard as stone
mysteries elusive as love
whispering to the encroaching dusk
psalms of heaven and earth

Fog | February 2009

When fog shrouds the lake
the sun hides his face
in linens of haze
Chautauqua forgets its name

Trees become blind men tapping their canes
waves disappear in dreamland mist
invisible fliers echo above

A ghost wrapping its robe
around invisible men
that is the lake when the fog rolls in

Fog, the soul mate of all and none
fog, a nomad swallowing his tongue

Waves | July 2008

Looking past the black-eyed susans and tree-climbing rose
we watch waves roll endlessly towards shore,
breaking free of the lake onto skull-sized rocks
they return submissively to the place where they were born
each identical to the one that came before
each a scroll of lyrics unrolled upon the shore

Sitting by the bank
in colored Adirondack chairs
we listen to their chorus
a song of journey's end
surrendered to the air

Storm Solace | July 2010

Put out the cup
world swirling wild
primordial genius
elemental chide

Lightning blitz
war zone daze
torrid wind
horizon ablaze

Pounding bursts
imploding lungs
sonic thuds
malevolent drums

I'll drink from their fountains
furious unrest
a mere dousing of warmth
spewed upon my chest

Give me steel-fisted wind
bullet squall rain
thunderhead jeers
balm to my pain

Storms come as balms
buckets of peace
drowning monotony
that's drowning me

Night Wind | July 2005

Skittering clouds crisscross the sky
smoke signals from a hidden tribe
warrior wind pillaging the night,
trampling Chautauqua on ponies of darkness
hooves dissolve as they touch each wave

Night advances with quickening pace
ripping flags to shreds with mayhem spears
slicing leaves from trees that breathe life into sky
scalping light from distant stars

The rampage hastens upon furious winds
the shaman moon blessing their raid
no one smokes the peace pipe tonight

County Chautauqua | May 2008

Chautauqua County
few outsiders know
this secret hideaway
a treasure hidden in the hills

Far from the noise of Buffalo
Syracuse and Albany
few hear its echo rustling
through the trees

The runt of the litter
among the economies of New York
bestowed with rivers and streams
strong in the face of adversities

Winds are alive in this county
more than in any other corner of the state
trees dance more vibrantly
than in any other space

The daylight sky is broad and wide
clouds painted on a canvas of blue
at night it wears a string of pearls
laced with silvery stars

Winter, spring and summer
baskets filled with wonders for everyone
and the spectacular colors of autumn
a prism of Chautauqua's sun

Hurricane Hunger | January 2014

An Atlantic hurricane hit
Chautauqua's shores
a crazy rage
stripping trees to skeletal soul

Sandy's voracious howl
spewed manic wind
like a pirate spitting
into the lake's spittoon

Appetite for destruction
unleashing mayhem,
razor rain slicing the air
gashing cheeks, biting ears
cutting through canvas
and jeans

The lake gagged,
a pot full of piss
choking on foam

Farther east
New York City
swelled

A dead cat
bobbed on the Hudson

Banks of Chautauqua | October 2007

A breeze of sparrows
shudders past my shoulder
alighting as one on the juniper
posted on the bank

Yarrow yellowing into autumn gold
ducks floating in morning nap
a woodpecker tapping its reveille
this is the spot where I find retreat

Legislature | November 2007

The legislature has convened
a parliament hatched
over fifty gulls in white
perched the length of Turner's patch

Laws have been passed
statutes for all to see
rulings of the council
dutifully confirmed
by whitewash decree

If yours is the lone dock standing
as a platform for caucusing the lake,
Chautauqua's birds will cast their votes
dropping edicts as enduring as paint

Bring a bucket, a scrub and scraping tool
the legislative branch of Chautauqua
has met and passed its rules

Autumn Evening | September 2013

Treetops lit by early evening glow
rise along Chautauqua's rim

A late season skier
slaloms the north shore
sheets of spray rise
peacock tails
against leaves of gold

Flags of Chautauqua | April 2008

The flags of Austria, Poland
Iceland and the US
fly at the end of my dock
standing tall over the lake's constant roll
unfurling themselves in freedom's wind

Three docks down
Sweden ascends
a tribute to ancestors who earlier
claimed Chautauqua as home

Canada, England and Indonesia
soar high above the banks of Lakewood
just beyond the Yacht Club
joining us all in fraternal bonds

On the edges of Ashville Bay
Germany and Brazil color the air
yellow, blue, red and green
proclaiming brotherhood for all to see

Finland and Italy join the chorus
stretching from Bemus
past Midway and Mission Meadows
past the banks of Dewittville
to the heart of Arnold's Bay

⋮
∨

These were the arms opened wide
the proud hands raised in sorrow
following a day of fear
September 11

These were the comforting voices heard
along the shores of Chautauqua
the day the world stood as one
against the terror of Ground Zero

Fall Specter | December 2008

He swims alone
to the center of the lake
Chautauqua his wayside
in the bleak wake of fall

A shadow cast in coal
feathers of pitch
smokestack neck
he floats as night
upon the shortened day

A pincher beak of black
his throat as long as his wings
he roams, a phantom
snaring wayward fish

In wide arc from my spot on land
I see him swim away
his compass eye tracking my moves
as I approach the bank

The double-crested cormorant
caped in ghostly soot
dives deep into the sky gray lake
and as silently as he curses my name
he is gone

October 1 | July 2014

Magical evening
trees in fall color
waves painted with sunset blush
muskies skulking through the weeds
waiting to take my bait

I troll along a drop-off
slowly
my lure spinning behind

Damn!
it's October 1
my fishing license expired yesterday

Pole in!
or the DNR could
confiscate my stuff
a thousand dollars of tackle at stake
glad I brought my notebook and pen

Never sure I will hook a fish
but, always certain
I'll find a poem floating on the waves

As swells of evening glow
rock my craft,
I realize there's more in this lake
than fish I hope to catch

Passing the Torch | October 2008

Skimming Chautauqua's surface
the crisp edge of fall gives notice
soon all will not be well for those
who try the patience of this lake

A straggler gull in solo flight
surveys endless waves,
his wings offering homage
to the sun's gradual retreat

Clouds that rose high in summer's arms
now slither at heightened speed
along tree lines abandoning green,
leaves flaunting the colors of death

Still, with death comes life
unlikely friends forever linked,
we too must suffer loss
as passage to a better world

The torch is being passed
the corpse is beginning to smoke
we must resolve our argument with
the present year
we have no other choice
we have no other hope

Tribute to an Old, Old Ash | December 2007

He's lying there on his side
a great beast of a tree
he fell at three-thirty this afternoon
the sun was shining
late October air crisp

We tried to count the rings
he was there long before the house was built
probably since around 1870
maybe longer

I didn't want to take him down
but, his limbs had become brittle
some threatening to fall the seventy feet to the ground
he was just too close to the house

I didn't mind that he imposed himself
between the patio and the lake
the yard was his long before it was ours
he was my companion while I wrote poems
into the night

He was a home to the nuthatch that
climbed down his long trunk head first
and to the red squirrel that followed,
both in pursuit of seeds and nuts
my wife placed on the patio wall

⋮
ᵛ

When he fell, his giant girth hitting the ground,
the earth trembled, sadness gripped me
nuts that the red squirrel stored away for the winter
burst out of the great arm that was broken in the fall

As the hired hands that leveled him
started to dismember his many limbs,
I thought of my dad, passed away a year ago

There is a limit to life and a time to die
for an ash like this about 140
for each of us about 90
if we are lucky

He lies there
a leviathan of this world
a patriarch to us all
a majestic brother of creation
awaiting the chains saws that will come tomorrow
to complete what must be done

I look at the old shagbark hickory
that stands just twenty feet away
and the large aging oak in the neighbor's yard
realizing they have lost a friend

⋮
∨

The three of them must have grown up together
each of them reaching arms to the sky these many years
each of them breathing long in the wind
each of them unfolding leaves upon the sun

Now there are just the two of them
each of us have lost a friend,
together we grieve
together we honor the beautiful old ash
that stood tall on Chautauqua's shore

Canadians | October 2008

Demanding attention
squadrons cleave the air
arrows piercing north to south
feathers battering clouds

On the water
a winged armada
defiantly navigates swells
from October to first throes of ice

Like hockey sticks applauding a score
they beat wings upon the waves
staking their claim to Chautauqua
sharing it only with snow geese and swans

These invaders from the north
perform this ritual every year
announcing winter is coming
the change of seasons is near

A Season's End | October 2007

For the past few weeks
nights have dipped into the mid-forties
chilling the lake at its top
dropping needles of cold into its thick green chop

Though the sun returns
with warm hands during the day
Chautauqua cannot dismiss night's fingers
bristling along its spine

The air itself has undergone a change
each day relinquishing its right to light
a sun collapsing sooner into its bed
time dictating more hours to the dark
unrolled as a bedcover upon October

A few powerboats, still fewer sails
pound through waves white at their crests
a stronger wind probes the skin
through inadequate leather vests

Migrating birds increasing in number
dot the lake, looking like decoys
deceiving land dwellers that the lake is warm
and swimming a joy

⋮
ᵛ

With sadness that comes at this time each year
I tell my son, Jon, the dock must come out the boat lift taken in
to delay another week would sentence our flesh
to the bite of a colder and crueler Chautauqua

As we stretch wet suits tight against our skins
and immerse into liquid cold,
we know we are marking a season's end

Snow | June 2008

Yesterday, snow returned to Chautauqua
arriving with geese making a brief stop
as they journeyed south

But, unlike geese
our snow came silently
falling through the night
and first hours of dawn
floating as a trance
across lake and hills
mystery ringing each crystal chime
mysteries only the deaf could hear

As the snow touched ground
a great white bear fell asleep upon the land
his fur a wooly blanket
insulating the earth from the cold
that bit our hands

White Night | December 2007

November's first snow sparkles
jewels dropped from the moon

A crystal spell cast upon yews trimming the yard
dark green hands covered by mittens of white

Black arms of the hickory and maple ascend to the stars
silver fingers frosted by winter's light
bygone stumps esteemed as alabaster thrones

My own limbs extend to the sky
beseeching heaven for knowledge I have yet to know
and secrets I promise to keep

Late November | November 2008

Inspiration writhes in the snow
a long necked swan
left to die

Ghostly oracles heaped up on shore
plead with the lake to surrender its soul

The lake a wounded buck
struggling in cold tar
noose tightens
slaps of wind steal life
from its lungs

Barren trees
silent profanities
numbed by change
stripped of flesh

Stalwart yews bow to dogmas of snow
submission flailing in their chests

Cattaraugus and Chautauqua
puppet counties strangled by snow belts
heavy on their hills

Brittle limbs dangle
from November's frozen hands

Near Perfect | January 2009

A crystalline skim
coats the lake
winter's first freeze

Mirror
pristine, pure
framing lights silent
on the banks
diamonds flawless
in the night

Late November's foray into cold
cannot hold more than a day,
as snow resolves to rain
the lake refuses to grip

Changes in our lives
bite with wintry cold
still, we grow brighter, stronger
resilient to the seasons' turn
near perfect reflections
of One who makes us whole

Announcing Winter | November 2014

Though wind furiously berates hills
vexing trees, birds and beasts
the lake has slowed
under concussion cold

Where waves once smashed banks
with powerful surges,
undulating sludge now
crawls to shore

Winter is coming
lake effect snows drop their weight
into liquid lead

A mere four days ago
golfers charged through
Chautauqua Golf Club
seduced by sixty-six degrees
in a season-ending romp

Today
it is coated in white
pins the sole possessors of frosted greens
limbless trees flying flags of summer

⋮
∨

In one day
lakeside tamaracks forfeited green for gold
the next, all needles stripped away

And each Thanksgiving Day
my golfing buddy and I tee up
our old Titleists, Top Flites and Calloways
next to those same tamaracks
hitting perfect drives
into the frigid fairway of Lake Chautauqua

Whiteout | December, 2011

Mid-December
Lake Erie hovers over Chautauqua
a polar bear shaking out its paws

A whiteout in party array
a billion flakes adorned in lace
spruce crowned with crystal tiaras
maples and oaks donned in tuxedos
windless backs suited black
chests starched white

Gatecrashers enter the yard
does with fawns ghostly as snow
apparitions edging close
begging hors d'oeuvres from
bird feeders posted in the yard
salads from arbor vitae green
a table welcoming all

The banquet hall is draped
in seasonal fling
tree stump cakes covered in icing
the lake a ballroom of white

A formal affair
with all the pomp
arrogance and formality
some wish to forget

For others like me
the invitation is one
I cannot turn down

The Freeze | December 2007

The moment is jarring
wind that whipped waves
with mayhem all year
can no longer move the lake

Sheets of slush,
Chautauqua's floating barges,
join hands, coalescing
a membrane solid, tight
chained by the freeze
that seals their fate

The moment is surreal
tongues of January
lie stuck to posts of winter steel,
this graveyard of warmer months
suspended on death slabs of ice

The lake is in pain
its fists clenched against the bitter change
knees buckling before a chilling throne

Chautauqua lies unconscious
cold-cocked by the whack of frigid wind
bitten by the iron jaws of frozen air

Silent and suspended
the lake yearns
for the freedom of spring

Winter's Prison (Through Chautauqua's Eyes) | October 2013

I am blinded each year at this time
my eyes stunned by shards of light
photons scattered like broken glass
on shifting sheets of ice

As air congeals into solid mass
waves are banished from my skin
winds hang heavy
upon curtains of frigid steel

Imprisoned in silence
life suspends on a meat hook of cold
and I, like flesh
succumb to the freeze

Cold | March 2008

Cold cracks the egg's back
a brutal friend so close
it heaps finality
upon a weaker skin

Still I welcome the cold
the way it strips the heart naked
and unclothes the soul

I congratulate the knives with eyes
that pass through me
as though my body was a wisp of light
I applaud the panes of ice
that see me as I really am

When the air is cold
flesh becomes honest
blood becomes the sun within

Alone in this cocoon of oneself
deceit is unveiled
the voice of God poised
in crystals without flaw

In the clarity of cold
amazement and fear lay frozen in my sight
while Chautauqua dangles like a worm
on a hook of frigid calm

Cooper's Hawk | February 2014

Hidden in winter yew
a prince sits on his throne
wild in a civilized world

His eye a gyroscope
set in swiveling head
his sphere unaware
of this predator's dread

Spying sparrows and finch
hanging as prizes
in arms of the yew,
he spars with each moment
to swoop and attack

Without warning
wings flare
hideaway explodes
blurring snow and feathers
a sparrow skewered
on raptor talons

Every morning
our hawk holds court
pronouncing verdict
with razor-like gavel

Time's Boulevard | April 2008

Over the snow-crowned lake
a layer of fog has settled for the night
a walkway for the pale wink of the moon
slivering within the mist

I see shadows moving along this boulevard
visitors in strange pink glow
a vision of the future perhaps
a procession of those who will come

Time ignores limits of space
and boundaries of mortals like us
Chautauqua's sky with hidden eyes
sees beyond the years in which we live

January | January 2009

Chautauqua abandoned
a desert cloaked in white
January's foot heavy on its face

Beneath the barren freeze
all is still
fish strung on icicle hooks
weeds forced back into silt
zebra mussels shaking in their shells

This jailor of seasons
buries his key under a coat of snow
enforcing a sentence sanctioned by ice
chaining the year in manacles of cold

While January seizes the lake
with hypnotic grip,
Cooper's hawk spins a sifting eye
for sparrows, rabbits and mice
all silent but awake
waiting for a poem to rise from its crypt
in the cemetery lake

Ice Monsters | March 2008

There are monsters in the lake

Imprisoned in frozen tombs
they rattle their wintry cage
mammoths heaving against slabs
hardened hides splintering peace

The slightest shift of seasonal heat
rouses them from sleep,
they lumber out of hibernation
with suffocated moans

From Celoron to Bemus they pound their angst
churning in cold boil, drums from a grave
groaning beasts mired in ice
butting heads on iron walls
tusks straining against immovable floes

Chautauqua's herd is on a rampage
clashing in titanic heave
the cracked lake
evidence of pressing beasts

I hear bellows in the night
horde running scared
Spring nipping at their heels

Monsters in the lake!

Silver Night | April 2009

A silver night
cast in midnight blue
a tablet of ice
smooth as razor swipe

Barren trees, crystalline sprays
shimmering lace, moonlit glaze

Night skates upon glitter and sheen
a ballet on ice, surrounded by evergreens

February slumbers
unaware of changes drawing near
drifting in dreamboat night
under a moonlight chandelier

Chautauqua Oak | June 2008

The large old oak
in the yard next to ours
bears the scars of years
long in the wind
a burden of time
occupying half the sky

Testimony of strength
at the edge of adversity,
outliving struggles
other lake dwellers know,
living larger than all our years

Anchored by a bulwark trunk
plunging deep into the earth
he outlasts fierce storm blasts
and brands of scorching sun

When Chautauqua's summer squalls
shred the clouds and stalk the lake
the oak stands firm
his sturdy beams supporting the fallen sky

Patriarch of endurance
determined and proud
none can bring him down

⋮
ᴠ

When autumn descends upon trees
shaking wrists to drop their leaves
the oak is slow to loose his grip
conceding just acorns
nuggets of eternal youth
a legacy of his prime

Through January cold
he holds his leaves close
ornaments of pride
defying winter's intimidation

In February's final days
they fall to earth
stars take their place
as buds upon his boughs

With wild arms climbing
black into a whitened night
he is the strong man of wnter
the compassionate innkeeper
to creatures seeking a home

When spring returns
the resilient oak stands tall
a giant on Chautauqua's shore
arms naked, opened wide
welcoming the tests of
yet another year

Triad | October 2013

He was twenty years old
a Marine stationed in Afghanistan
last week they laid his body out
in Jamestown, New York
he returned home two weeks too soon

I remember Aaron as a gentle
responsible boy,
when we went on vacation
he would come over and
care for our dogs

She was a neighbor from my youth
living with her husband in Hawaii
they had found paradise
until cancer found her too

Claudia was a young wife
pregnant with her first child
I would watch her from my window
tenderly nurturing her garden

I received the news that both had died
the same week

⋮
∨

Aaron's life cut short by a mortar
in terror-ridden hills,
Claudia succumbed to another terrorist
in her early seventies
leaving three sons and
a grieving husband

That same week
the ice-burdened roof of the barn
housing my boat for the winter
collapsed
it didn't matter
I can get another boat